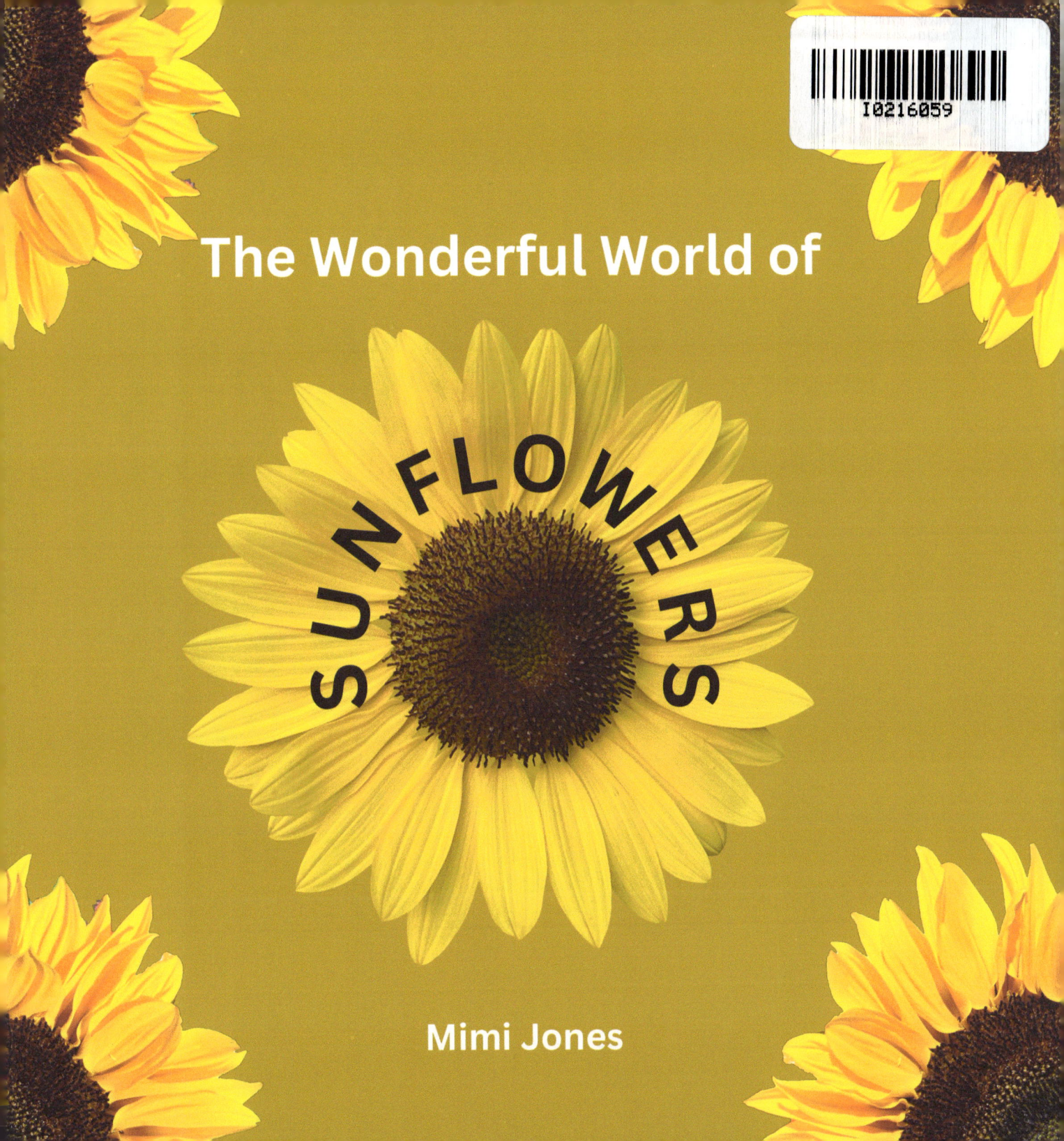

The Wonderful World of SUNFLOWERS

Mimi Jones

Dedicated to my beautiful sister!

All rights reserved.
No part of this book may be reproduced in any form or by any means, electronic or mechanical, and no photocopying or recording, unless you have written permission from the author.

ISBN 978-1-958985-10-6

Copyright © 2024 by Mimi Jones

www.joeysavestheday.com

A Mimi Book

Their scientific name comes from the Greek words helios (meaning sun) & anthos (meaning flower).

Sunflowers belong to the genus Helianthus.

There are over sixty species of flowering plants in the daisy family and sunflowers are one of those sixty.

Sunflowers are mostly native to North and South America.

Sunflowers always face the east in the morning waiting for the sun to shine.

Throughout the day the sunflowers will move towards the sun.

As the sun is setting in the west the sunflowers will have made a 180-degree turn towards the sun.

During the nighttime hours, the sunflowers turn back towards the east so when the sun rises they will get all the warm sunshine.

The pattern continues east to west until the sunflowers age, and are unable to move anymore.

This process is known as heliotropism.

The common sunflower (Helianthus annuus) has impressive flower heads which can be up to 12 inches wide in cultivated types.

Sunflowers come in various colors, including yellow, red, orange, maroon, and brown.

Yellow is the most common color.

The tallest sunflower
ever grown reached
30 feet and 1 inch.
It was grown by
Hans-Peter Schiffer
who resides in Germany.

Depending on the variety, sunflowers are ready for harvest within 80 to 120 days from planting.

At the end of the sunflower season,
the sunflowers are harvested,
and the seeds are dried out.

Once the seeds have been dried out and prepared people may eat them. Sunflower seeds are sold in many stores around the world.

Sunflower seeds are packed with calcium, making them a perfect healthy snack.

Bees and butterflies love sunflowers. They carry pollen from one sunflower to another.

Pollination is what helps produce the seeds in the sunflower.

Sunflowers can be annuals or perennials, depending on which species the sunflower is.

Annuals only grow once. Perennials can grow back the following year.

The wild sunflower is the official state flower for Kansas.

 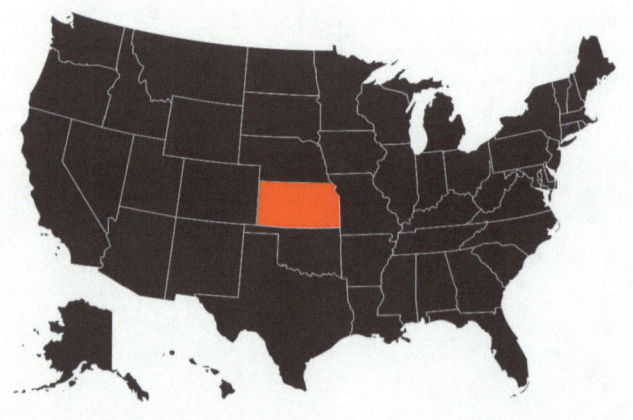

Sunflowers are the national flower for both Russia and the Ukraine.

Russian Flag

Ukrainian Flag

Sunflowers need more than 6 to 8 hours of sunlight every day to stay healthy.

In a sun-kissed meadow, where the grass whispered secrets to the wind, there stood a solitary sunflower named Sunny.

Sunny was no ordinary flower; she had a voice that could rival the sweetest songbirds. Sunny loved to sway back and forth to her own melody.

And so, dear reader, if you ever chance upon a sunflower swaying in the breeze, listen closely. You might hear the echo of Sunny's song—a reminder that even in fleeting moments, beauty leaves its mark.

Remember, sunflower fields are not only beautiful they play a vital role in wildlife conservation and provide delightful photo opportunities.

Go make lots of memories!

www.ingramcontent.com/pod-product-compliance
Lightning Source LLC
Chambersburg PA
CBHW042133070426
42453CB00002BA/73